You Know You're Over 40 When . . .

Written by Herbert I. Kavet
Designed and Illustrated by Martin Riskin

First Printing August 1982
Second Printing March 1983
Third Printing July 1983
Fourth Printing September 1983

1

About the Author:

Herbert Kavet was educated on a Monopoly Board at PS 193 in Brooklyn where his chief extra curricular activity was peeking up little girls dresses on the open stair wells. Later as an engineer, he designed a multitude of bridges, roads, and other structures, none of which were ever built. His present activities consist mainly of working out at various sports and looking in mirrors in a valiant attempt to resurrect his 40 year old body.

About the Artist:

The less said about the artist the better. Senior Martin Riskin developed his early art style carving obscenities on desk tops at Chelsea public schools. He later specialized in recording artistic perversions on restroom walls. He wouldn't be mentioned at all in a high class book of this sort, but he threatened the author with a sharpened pencil.

Published simultaneously in Canada by
Encore Sales Inc. of Downsview, Ontario.

Manufactured in the United States of America.

IVORY TOWER PUBLISHING COMPANY, INC.
125 Walnut Street, Watertown, Massachusetts 02172
TEL: (617) 923-1111   TELEX: 955-439 Intel. Div. - ITOP

INTRODUCTION

I shouldn't even be writing this book. Most people think I'm only 27 or so. Why just the other day, some girl (ahem) woman thought I was joking when I mentioned the Class of 1958. "Middle Age" as you know is anyone ten years older than you and I certainly don't fall into **that** group.

Then again, some college "kids" are starting to call me Mister. Perhaps that is what started this little guide; someone had to enumerate all the signs that really tell you when You're Over 40 - Just in case you look so young that everyone else forgets.

APOLOGY

You may notice that this book is written almost entirely from a male point of view. This was not an accident. Our research shows that most women seldom pass the age of 40. The curious nature of this phenomenon will be studied further in the sequel to this volume entitled "Bifocals Aren't That Bad".

You Know You're Over 40 When...

You feel like the morning after and you can swear
you haven't been anywhere.

You Know You're Over 40 When . . .

You start wearing Boxer Shorts instead of the "Jockey" type. You notice colored underwear in the ads but yours are all white.

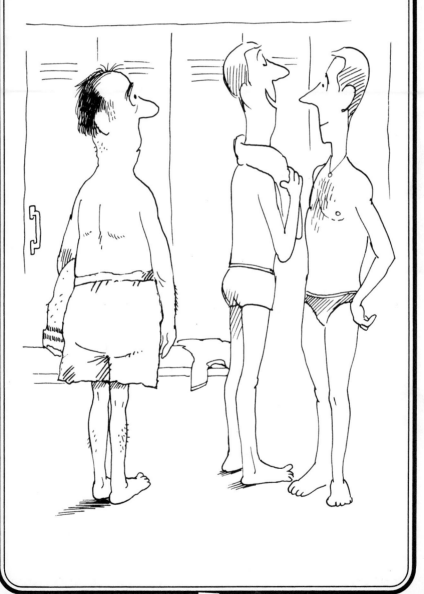

You Know You're Over 40 When . . .

You think "Gay" means jolly, cheerful, and vivacious.

You Know You're Over 40 When . . .

You go to a school reunion and everyone looks sooo OLD.
All your classmates are overweight.
You can't believe they have co-ed dorms now.

You Know You're Over 40 When . . .

You learn to control your drinking—you even start doing things that are good for yourself like eating yogurt. You read can labels for cholesterol content.

You start to observe speed limits - you may even pay $10,000 for a restored MG that cost $1500 new when you were in college.

You Know You're Over 40 When . . .

You finally realize that your mother isn't
the greatest cook in the world.
At least she remembers that you hate string beans.

You Know You're Over 40 When . . .

Instead of combing your hair, you start "arranging" it. There is more hair on your chest than on your head. Some of your friends grow beards on their chins to camouflage the loss on the top part of their heads.

You Know You're Over 40 When . . .

Some of the Presidents you actually voted
for were later shown to be such incompetents
that you are totally ashamed to tell anyone.

You Know You're Over 40 When . . .

You stop to think and sometimes forget to start again.
You appreciate the luxury of a nap in front of the TV.

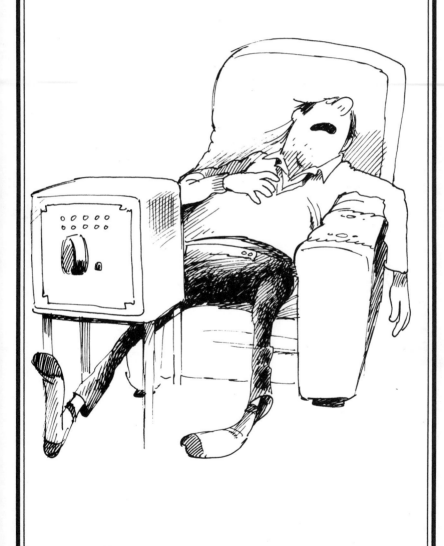

You Know You're Over 40 When . . .

You start entering Senior, Master and Veteran class sport events - and STILL lose.

You Know You're Over 40 When . . .

Work becomes more fun and fun becomes more work.

You still have an 8% mortgage that you once thought was too high. Your house has increased in value, an amount equal to the National Debt.

You Know You're Over 40 When . . .

You start reading the ads for Hemorrhoids, Constipation, Hair Loss, and various pain relievers. You begin buying the stuff - worse, it helps.

You Know You're Over 40 When . . .

You stop making excuses for sexual malfunction and realize you're tired. You turn out the lights for economic reasons instead of romantic ones.

You Know You're Over 40 When . . .

You start examining your life goals, objectives and achievements and realize you're not making ANY of them.

You can no longer help the kids with their homework. On the parts you help with, they get "C−".

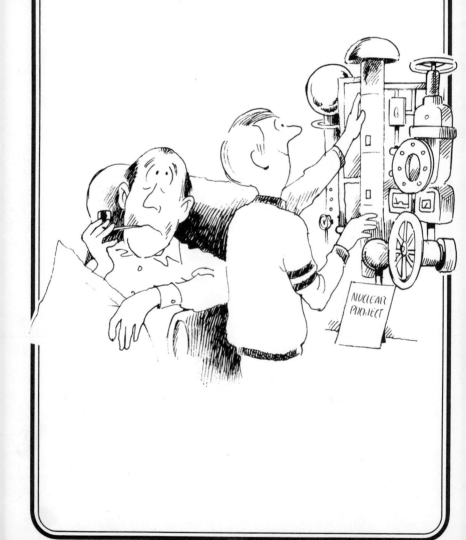

You Know You're Over 40 When . . .

Getting a little action means your prune juice is working.

You Know You're Over 40 When . . .

You start to notice the ages of people in the news like politicians
and company presidents - and they're younger than you.
Your doctor is also younger than you.

You Know You're Over 40 When . . .

You start calculating how many years you have left, rather than how old you are. You start taking retirement plans seriously. You stop looking forward to birthdays.

You really have to concentrate to call "Girls", "Women".
You remember when calling Women, "Girls" was a compliment.

You participate in a ball game on Sunday
and hurt until Wednesday.

You Know You're Over 40 When . . .

Your kids are bigger than you and you start saying things to them like, "When I was your age . . .", that you hated when your father said them to you.

You realize certain foods just aren't compatible with your gastro intestinal system. You develop a taste for Bran Flakes.

Some of your neckties are wide and some are narrow, and you can't quite remember the sequence of which width was in or out and when.

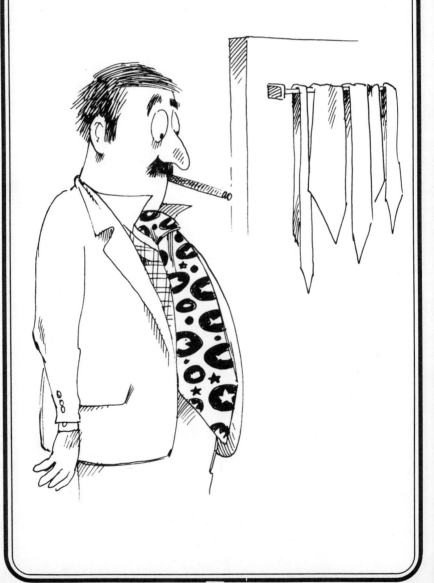

You Know You're Over 40 When . . .

You think "grass" is something you cut, and "snorting coke" is sucking cola up your nose through a straw.
When you hear about drugs—you think of penicilin.

You Know You're Over 40 When . . .

You give up smoking because it's bad for you and stick to it for six days longer than when you gave it up last time.

You Know You're Over 40 When . . .

You start to fantasize about career changes, but don't dare make a move. Your boss may be younger than you - worse HE may be a SHE.

You Know You're Over 40 When . . .

College-aged people start calling you MISTER.

You Know You're Over 40 When . . .

You start calling anyone under 30, "KIDS".

You Know You're Over 40 When . . .

It takes you all night to do what you used to do all night.

You Know You're Over 40 When . . .

Your kids start to beat you in your best sport. Then they find excuses to avoid playing with you. You need more time outs.

You Know You're Over 40 When...

You find almost any young woman extremely attractive. You can find some physically redeeming quality in any 20 year old.

You Know You're Over 40 When . . .

You realize your contemporaries are
ALL making more money than you.

You Know You're Over 40 When . . .

You really need a cocktail before 6:00 p.m. In fact on most days, 4:00 would be much more reasonable.

You Know You're Over 40 When...

Professional athletes seem to look younger and younger. So do policemen. You are shocked at the youths in military uniforms that you see. "Why, they're just KIDS".

You think Club Med is some sort of camp for retired doctors.

You Know You're Over 40 When . . .

You realize your father was right when he said it's as easy to fall in love with a rich girl as a poor one.

You go to a party and everyone looks middle-aged. You get invited to a 50's party and you have twelve possible "costumes" still in your closet.

You Know You're Over 40 When . . .

Your favorite songs were played on the Lawrence Welk Show.

Most of your friends are divorced and are busy developing a new life style.

You Know You're Over 40 When . . .

Your kids are big enough to wear your clothes, but they wouldn't be caught dead in them.

You Know You're Over 40 When...

You're cold. You start dressing much warmer than younger people.
You can't believe "kids" are outside wearing only a sweater
and you're freezing wearing a hat, jacket, overcoat and gloves,
and you're still in the car.

You Know You're Over 40 When . . .

A boy scout offers you a seat on a bus or subway.

You Know You're Over 40 When . . .

When you find yourself on virtually every junk mail list in the country. During the Christmas season alone you get 43 full color catalogs *everyday.*

You start to take the Surgeon General seriously.

You Know You're Over 40 When . . .

You go to a stag party and are the only one sober enough to even think of driving home.

You Know You're Over 40 When . . .

Your daughter's friends have better figures than your wife. If you try to "swing" with a cute young thing, the waitress asks if she is your daughter.

You Know You're Over 40 When . . .

You learn the pronunciation of 3 white wines, well enough to order them without risking a waiter's snicker.

You Know You're Over 40 When . . .

You can still sing the Howdy Doody and Mouseketeers songs.

You Know You're Over 40 When . . .

You can eat a double chocolate fudge sundae and not get any pimples.

You Know You're Over 40 When . . .

You let your Playboy subscription lapse.

You Know You're Over 40 When . . .

You're turned down for a special low rate life insurance policy.

You Know You're Over 40 When...

Everyone can beat you on video and computer games.

You still have a 3-speed bike. Should you buy a 10-speed job, you would only use it twice.

You Know You're Over 40 When . . .

You take up jogging and no matter how fast or far you run there is always some big mouth around who runs faster and farther.

You Know You're Over 40 When . . .

After a free trial at a *coed* health club you sign up for the 5-year special.

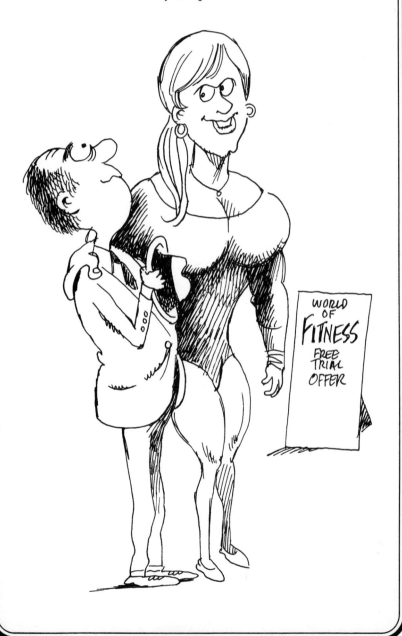

You Know You're Over 40 When . . .

Sometimes you sit down to put on your underwear.

You Know You're Over 40 When . . .

You find yourself starting sentences with "Years ago," or "When I was a boy."

You Know You're Over 40 When . . .

You spy a rather plain looking older guy on a boat 3 times the size of yours surrounded by several young beauties, and you know *exactly* what they see in him.

TINYTANIC

You Know You're Over 40 When . . .

When your Mother-in-Law finally stops looking at you as though you are always *ravishing* her daughter.

You Know You're Over 40 When . . .

When your kids college tuition for *one* semester would have been enough to endow a new gymnasium at the time you were a student.

You Know You're Over 40 When . . .

You visit your mother and she tells you to put on a hat or rubbers or to eat more pot roast and you do it without an argument just to make her happy.

You Know You're Over 40 When . . .

You join some "kids" singing at a bar or party and none of them know the words to your drinking songs.

You Know You're Over 40 When . . .

You buy a new suit and the salesman asks if you want cuffs or not and you don't have the foggiest idea of which is in and which is out this year. You have even less idea of whether your trousers are supposed to "break" over your shoes (or are boots back in style?).

You Know You're Over 40 When . . .

You listen patiently to your father's old stories and pretend to be as interested as can be because you love him.

You Know You're Over 40 When . . .

You wake up without an alarm clock before 7:00 each day; and the best part of your day is already over.

You Know You're Over 40 When . . .

Everything hurts — what doesn't hurt, doesn't work.

You know all the answers but the kids won't ask you the questions.

You Know You're Over 40 When . . .

You start forgetting. People inform you of this often enough that you sometimes wonder if all your marbles are there.

You Know You're Over 40 When . . .

You switch from "Levis" to "Action Jeans".

You Know You're Over 40 When . . .

Anything under 25¢ isn't worth bending over for.

You drink Pepsi to quiet your stomach and not to become a member of the Pepsi Generation.

You switch from a double bed to Twin size.

You Know You're Over 40 When . . .

You start mixing up the names of your kids or other relatives. You need a calculator to figure out their birthdays.

You Know You're Over 40 When . . .

You remember how hard it was to "Score" with a "girl" who wore a girdle.

You've never been in a hot tub or isolation chamber. If you have been in a hot tub its been with your wife.

You Know You're Over 40 When . . .

You're getting a little thin on top and your wife is getting a little thick on the bottom.

You Know You're Over 40 When . . .

Your back hurts. Following the advice of 27 different doctors, friends, osteopaths and chiropracters, you change your mattress, shoes, posture, car seats, you lose weight, wear a brace, rest in bed, and do exercises, and give up 3 favorite sports, and it still hurts.

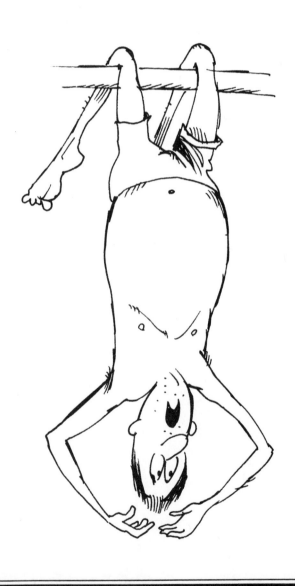

You Know You're Over 40 When . . .

You can't believe you hear yourself telling the "kids" at the office "we tried that and it didn't work".

You Know You're Over 40 When . . .

You grow pleased with your pear shaped figure finding it both attractive and aerodynamically sound.

You find it much more rewarding to watch your kids excel at some sport than to play yourself and risk tearing yourself apart.

You Know You're Over 40 When . . .

You're smart enough not to test your strength by taking out all the garbage cans at one time.

You Know You're Over 40 When . . .

You no longer sleep like a baby. Sometimes you have trouble falling asleep, sometimes you awake in the middle of the night and sometimes you wake up much too early in the morning. You can still, however, sleep through almost any sermon.

You Know You're Over 40 When . . .

You think "making it" is kissing in the back seat of a car.

You Know You're Over 40 When . . .

You are ready to drop everything and have a beer while participating in any strenuous activity. Come to think of it, you were ready to drop anything and have a beer when you were 20 also.

You Know You're Over 40 When . . .

You may not be as good as you once were, but you're as good once as you ever were.

You Know You're Over 40 When . . .

You think "Plato's Retreat" is a cave in which the Greek Philosopher meditated.

You Know You're Over 40 When . . .

You call "Tennis Shoes" and "Running Shoes" SNEAKERS.
When the sporting goods stores called them sneakers they cost
$4.95 and not $54.00.

Things you grew up with and used as a kid are becoming collectibles. You wish you had saved your Mickey Mouse watch.

Time passes so much faster than when you were a child. Weekends arrive quickly, seasons pass one after another, your kids suddenly grow up and then one day . . .

Someone throws a surprise birthday party and all your friends come and they bring you gag gifts that poke fun at various parts of you.